Julia's Story

By
Julia Fuhrman Craig

Julia's Story

By Julia Fuhrman Craig

Copyright © 2023 Julia Fuhrman Craig

All rights reserved. No part of this book may be reproduced or transmitted in any form or by any means electronic or mechanical including photocopying, recording, or by any information storage and retrieval system without permission in writing from the publisher or Author.

Aurora Books, an imprint of Eco-Justice Press, L.L.C.

Aurora Books
P.O. Box 5409 Eugene, OR 97405
www.ecojusticepress.com

ISBN: 978-1-945432-58-3
Library of Congress Control Number: 2023934407

Dedication

To my two adult children Farley and Garrit Craig

Contents

Introduction

1. Early Beginning 1948-1949

2. Chapman Bailey Studio

3. Chinatown, Los Angeles 1950

4. Country Homes

5. Maxine's Fabrics

6. My Marriage

7. Awakening 1986

8. Mother's Goodness

9. Laura Julia Baskett and Charlie Columbus Baskett 1868-1968

10. Christian Science/ Carl Jung

11. New Life New Awareness

12. Mother's Passing

13. The Journal And Photo Discovery

14. Putting The Pieces Together

15. Secrets Seep

Introduction

When I was still in high school, sitting in English class on a hot Southern California Spring afternoon, listening to Mr. Manus reading an Edna Saint Vincent Millay poem, "We Were Very Merry". I told myself that I would be a writer when I grew up. I wasn't by any means his star pupil, nor did he even know my name in that crowded baby boomer class. However, I had no idea at the time that my life would extend out to be a fascinating story that I was meant to write and share. Today I am 76 and have been working on this story as it has unfolded before me for many years. I changed the names of my two sisters to protect their privacy.

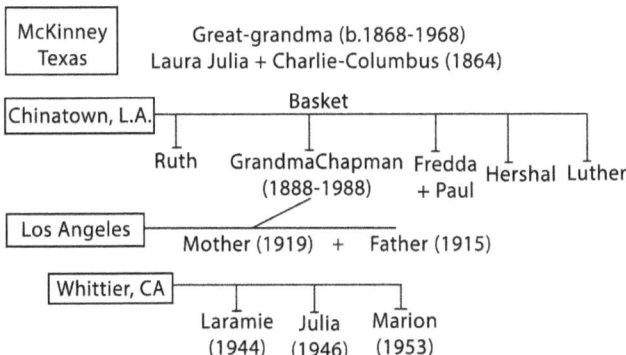

Chapter 1
Early Beginning

I was born in 1946 in Los Angeles. We moved back to Los Angeles from Navy housing in Palo Alto when I was three. My father was an Annapolis Graduate Naval Submarine Officer in World War II and although he had hoped to go into the airline industry upon return from war, our mother persuaded him to join her lucrative family business of importing and selling chinaware and chinaware painting supplies: Chapman-Baily Studios. We moved into the large apartment above the now second-generation business which was then housed in a white Victorian house on the busy Beverly Blvd., downtown Los Angeles, while we waited for our country home to be built in nearby Orange County. My sister Laramie was two years older than I. There were four of us in the family currently.

My mother married my father just before World War II. My mother who was born in 1919, was brunette, petite, beautiful, red lipstick lips, from a relatively wealthy family who had a home on Balboa Island, a mountain cabin, and a lovely home with maid's quarters in upscale downtown Los Angeles.

Of course, my father was charmed by our mother's family. He was born in Fort Thomas, Kentucky in 1915, into a modest family, their only child. His parents eventually lived in an apartment in Cincinnati, Ohio—they never owned home nor a car. They were so proud of his Annapolis achievement, but disappointed that he chose to marry and live on the West Coast, two thousand miles away from them.

Julia's Story

I heard that our mother wasn't the kindest date, but was available to my handsome, Navy Officer dad, even though she stood him up at times, and did not go out of her way to meet his parents in the East when she was traveling there. I was not living then—but I do know that getting a husband was a paramount task for young women whose men were sent to war. He was not her first choice, but seemed to be a viable choice, so they married just before he went off to war, January 22, 1942. Submarine Officers and mates were not notorious survivors, one in three never returned, but our dad returned. Their first child, my sister Laramie was born November 1944. He first met her when she was one year old. I was born two years later. Eventually, my parents had one more daughter Marion in 1953.

This was our LA beginning. Chapman-Baily Studios was a business my mother's paternal grandmother Julia Chapman established at the turn of the century, because her blacksmith husband had been murdered one night in downtown Los Angeles, after he sold a horse at an auction, and was carrying the money home. He left her with two deaf boys to raise on her own. The boys were deafened by scarlet fever. The younger of the two was to be my grandfather.

So, in 1949, we moved into the upper apartment of the family business, downtown LA, on a terribly busy downtown LA Beverly Blvd.

I need to tell you at this point, that this book is titled *Julia's Story* for a reason. Both of my sisters Laramie and Marion have different stories than I do. As a sister, I was close with neither of them.

Chapter 2
Chapman-Baily Studio 1900-1986

My father gave up his full Navy retirement seven years early to work in my mother's family business. My first embedded memory of our new home above the business was of the day and night ambulance sirens screaming up and down the boulevard below our apartment to the nearby LA Hospital. I had never experienced such a ruckus!

Several cement steps lead up from the 2-lane Beverly Boulevard to the covered porch of the business that was housed in a large, old white two-story Victorian house. A heavy oak front glassed-door with the name "Chapman-Baily Studios" painted on the glass in gold paint sat at the top of the porch stairs. A shiny brass-plated handle with keyhole was set into the wooden door above the handle.

Our new home entry, the upstairs apartment door was much narrower and on the far left of the covered porch. It opened into a wooden staircase to the apartment where the tall rooms smelled of fresh oil-based paint. Our voices echoed in this deep stairwell as we noticed the cool stagnant air filling our lungs. My sister and I shared a large light-blue bedroom with two single beds. Mother and Daddy's bedroom was wallpapered in purple lilac blooms on one wall at the head of their double bed. The kitchen was a make-shift variety made of white enamel movable Sears kitchen cupboards and sink. There was a large dining room with heavy wood table, wooden chairs and a day bed. The adjacent, empty living room was eventually furnished with an early version of a black and white television where we watched *Howdy Doody* and *Melton Burl* as we sat on the wooden floor.

Once we settled into the apartment, each morning, Daddy would help dress Laramie and I and fix our soft-boiled egg breakfasts, in a white eggcups decorated with a blue Navy anchor emblems—before he went downstairs to work in the shop with our grandfather, while our mother slept in.

Laramie and I had little supervision. We roamed the clove-oil scented china shop—the scent wafting from Grandfather's kiln firings. All shapes of white chinaware were stacked on display tables in the shop. . . . plates, teacups, tea pots, trays, vases. Painted display pieces with pansies, iris, and roses hung on the walls and sat upright on shelves in order to woo customers into china painting ideas.

I would sometimes sit on the wooden floor of the shop, lining up the china animal-shaped salt and pepper shakers to form a parade (chickens, pigs, cats, turkeys, cows) or I would sit on the floor surveying the open file drawer of tiny, corked glass vials containing powdered china paint. I'd pick out my favorite colors: Dusty Rose, Lemon Yellow, and Robin Egg Green.

My sister Laramie and I were only told—do not cross the dangerous, busy boulevard, nor go down the gravel alley next to the business where bad people live. So, we played hide and seek in the back yard under the crabapple tree where grandpa stored dozens of tarp-covered wooden crates from the orient that were stuffed with white china pieces cushioned in wood-shaving excelsior. Large Japanese symbols were written in black paint on each crate. These bigger than us crates, for playing, plus other adventures called to us as we played about unsupervised.

Next to this hide 'n seek haven was a horse-barn-turned-warehouse. The smaller supply items for the store, such as powdered paint and paint brushes, pallets and pallet knives were stored inside, alongside the red, winding, creaky barn staircase that led up to Grandpa's room with naked lady calendars hanging from a beam—the first of which I had ever seen.

When I wandered inside the store, I'd sometimes hear my grandmother Chapman shout to our Grandpa Burk, "Take this order out to the customer's car!" She rarely spoke to him in a soft tone as he was nearly stone deaf, his left ear was plugged with a hearing aid from which the wires hung leading to the battery in his left shirt pocket. At times, the device would squeal out a terrifying sound until Grandmother motioned for him to tend to it.

Once when Laramie and I dropped a brick from our second story apartment porch to the ground behind the business below, Grandpa Burk yelled to us, "You kids stop that"!

I do not remember him ever speaking to us other than that day. And we'd only notice a glimmer of joy in his blank face when he picked up his Siamese cat "Smoke" by the nap of his neck to display him to us all stretched out or when he found and shared a monster-faced squash or anomaly Siamese-twin tomatoes from his vegetable patch. He might have also given out a slight chuckle at these times. These were his small pleasures. Sometimes he would go out fishing on a charter boat and come back with ogle-eyed grotesque fish wrapped in newspaper. He'd chuckle and wince as he unwrapped them and showed them to us.

I went with him once when he walked through the neighborhood collecting the rent money from the houses he and Grandmother Chapman owned. When one memorable older lady tenant opened her front door to us, I was stricken with an odd, thick sweetness pouring over me. Today I wonder if it had been the sweet smell of opium.

Another of his tenants, Old Mrs. Eckhart, lived in the attic of a house bordering our crabapple tree, crate-filled back yard. Sometimes we could hear her banging around in her screen porch kitchen. On occasion, Laramie and I would climb the tall wooden stairs leading up to her door and knock. She would greet us always with a welcome smile and invite us in. She often gave us little sacks of ribbon Christmas candy or secondhand children's books. She was a kind old soul, we were told, even though she took in all the alley cats and her apartment smelled bad—our father thought.

Before we moved away to our new home in the country by Uncle Paul, she returned the Christmas gift mother had given her for babysitting us once—red ribbon still intact and box unopened. She would not take money or gifts for babysitting us once.

smoke   Granpa

Chapter 3
Chinatown Los Angeles, 1950

Chapman-Baily Studio, was less than a mile away from Chinatown, LA. At this early time of 1949 in LA when we first moved to the apartment above the business, we often went to General Lee's famous Chinatown Restaurant. Grandmother Chapman's family included her husband, our grandpa, her mother who was our great-grandmother Laura, Julia Basket, as well as her two sisters—maiden Auntie Ruth and Auntie Fredda along with Uncle Paul, Fredda's husband. They all met us there. I was unaware that Grandmother's two brothers our Uncle Herschel and Uncle Luther, and her father Charlie Columbus Baskett had all passed in three different recent instances around 1946-1948.

We were not of Chinese descent, no matter, it was as if we belonged there in some manner. I remember eventful dinners there for several years—my parents, my sister Laramie and I. The six elders made us ten in all.

My dad would park our light-green convertible 1948 Chevy in a parking lot; then he would pay the attendant twenty-five cents, and we would walk under the green pagoda roof of the West Gate which was outlined in brilliant white neon lights that defined the dancing roof tips of the gate. Substantial Chinese-red painted metal posts held up this brilliant neon entrance gate.

Chinatown Plaza lay beyond the gate and our first stop was usually to the organ grinder man by the wishing pool—who was playing his herty-gerty, and holding the leash of his little monkey. The monkey wore a felt hat and a vest with large pockets. Daddy would give Laramie and I each a coin to hold out to the little monkey, holding them out flat in front of us as we watched this sweet little monkey come over to gently scrape his fingers over our offering hands. He'd then put the coins in his sagging oversized vest pocket, tip his elastic chinstrap hat, glance to his master for a quick approval, then ready himself for the next offering. The mere touch of his fragile fingers brushing over mine filled me with squealing delight.

The six elder family members often joined us at the monkey grinder before we ascended the stairway to General Lee's second-story restaurant. There was no elevator, so my forever enduring 83-year-old Great-grandmother Laura Julia made the trek up the stairs with a little help from her son-in-law our Great Uncle Paul.

Once inside the tall red Chinese double doors of General Lee's that was marked with black Chinese characters, we were graciously greeted by a bowing host, then seated at our formally reserved long rectangular table. The table was covered with a starched white tablecloth on which stood starched stand-up white cloth napkins and lowlit candles in red glass containers.

Numbers of busy Chinese waiters in red knot/buttoned long sleeved Chinese shirts along with black tie-up loose pants, wearing little flat black hats, waited on us. Our little china teacups were quickly filled with boiling hot green tea and our water glasses with tingling icy water. Great-grandmother Laura Julia sitting at the head of the table with our grandmother Chapman to her left side. They conversed and easily ordered a dozen separate pedestal dishes for all of us to enjoy family-style.

Cups of hot yellow egg-flower soup topped with thin slices of green onion were next served to each of us. I noticed my Chinese soup spoon could be tipped back so that the soup ran down the scooped handles to burn my fingers if I was not careful. How I delighted in this discovery, not to mention the chopsticks at each place setting. I watched my great-grandmother and others around her—how strangely adept at using chopsticks.

Short as I was, seated at table-top eye level, I watched my grandfather pour spoon after spoon of sugar into his tea. Naturally, I had to follow suit. My sister and I were soon invisibly forgotten once we were seated, and the intense adult conversation of serious family matters and current politics ensued at the other end of the table. I watched the evening unfold from this lower table-top view, as I entertained myself with soup spoon, chopsticks and sugar-laden tea.

The steaming dishes came to us on covered china pedestal plates. There were pork short ribs, chow mien, egg foo young, egg rolls, steamed sesame vegetables, deep fried shrimp, sweet and sour chicken and mounds of white and fried rice. Each dish was passed around and around the long table until the platters were nearly empty, then, Grandfather would usually scrape off every leftover tidbit morsel onto his own plate as a last rite.

The din air of the busy dark Chinese restaurant entranced us with another time and place. After we were finished and could not eat another bite, the Chinese waiter brought us a plate of fortune cookies. We listened to our fortunes being read aloud by a nearby family member elder, Uncle Paul. Great-grandmother paid the bill with cash. Then we would slowly disembark, putting the well-used starched napkins back on the table, and gradually walk toward the entrance doors to begin our descent down toward the plaza, as the impeccable Chinese waiters bowed silently toward us to honor our presence.

Grandmother Chapman was quite familiar with the Phoenix Bakery down on the Plaza and would lead us there where she bought a dozen deep fried honey-dipped and twisted "butterflies" along with almond cookies and rock candy for all of us to somehow manage to down a dessert cookie, candy or both.

Little did I know that five decades or more before our Chinatown dinners, my Great-grandmother Laura Julia raised her five children in a tiny, rented bungalow just a few blocks away on a hilly street called Bernardo Street. At a much later date, Grandmother Chapman commented to me that when she was in high school, they were so poor they had no living room furniture. Her sister Fredda made mention of the long braided Chinese cues that the Chinese men wore down their backs in honor of the Chinese Emperor, that she remembered.

I also had no idea that they had lived in Chinatown. . . nor, that there was so much more to their story.

Chapter 4
Country Homes

Before our new country home next to Great Uncle Paul and Great Auntie Fredda, was finished we would drive out to the construction site on the weekends to watch the progress of the building site. I only remember picking up the metal slugs that the electrician has tossed on the unfinished floors, thinking they were nickels and could fit into the trinket machines at the grocery store.

The house site was on an acre that my parents bought from Great Uncle Paul. It was adjacent to his own two-acre farm and fruit orchard. Once we moved into the new home, Uncle Paul became part of our life. Great Uncle Paul was once a cowboy in his youth, but now he was bald, and so thin his grey work pants buckled at the waist under his tightened belt. Average size, he wore a semi-permanent smile of kindness. He was child-like and was always available to invite Laramie and I over to pick ripe peaches berries, figs, apricots, or watch him behead chickens for Sunday dinner, watch him boil their feathers off and gut them, or take us on a ride in his wooden garden cart on a fantasy journey of his own making, like a Disney tour guide way before Disney even set down the first stake at nearby Disneyland. We sat inside the cart, he pulled while he'd narrate the journey, "Now we are going into the deep forest, the coolest place in Southern California" as he wheeled us under his tiny grove of three Pine trees.

Often when we were children with mother visiting Paul and Fredda in their parlor, Paul was asked to escort us out to pick fruit so the adults could continue their conversations in private. Or should it be raining , he was told to take us in the living room to play with the blocks and school supplies Auntie Fredda took home upon retirement. Auntie Fredda met Paul at the Los Angeles elementary school where she taught for 25 years. He was the school custodian. She was petit, lively, her face now wrinkled and over-tanned by too many years gardening their two acres in the California sun. She always wore waist-less dresses that she made herself. She never wore pants or jeans. Her voice was school-teacher stern. One of her students, Micky Rooney, was her claim to fame. She remembers him organizing little side shows out on the playground.

Once, when I was five years old, I dared to take a grape off her table without asking, "No, put that back, you didn't ask me first!" she scolded. But when we visited their parlor, she was overgenerous with all the candy she kept in the top drawer of her mahogany high boy—raspberry chews, moth balls, caramel-twists, pastel candy-covered almonds, and chocolate peanut clusters. We could have all we wanted.

He and our grandmother's sister Great Auntie Fredda lived in a tall redwood sided gabled house surrounded by her abundant flower garden of magnolias, zinnias, and roses as well as his fruit orchard. They had no children of their own, so our nearby arrival may have been a blessing to them both.

We lived in this new country home next to Uncle Paul and Auntie Fredda—a path and a gate between our properties—until our mother became pregnant with our little sister Marion. It was explained to us that we had to get a bigger house, bigger than the two bedroom that they had built. So, we moved again, this time to nearby Whittier into a much bigger house in a more exclusive neighborhood. This is where I started third grade. It never occurred to me why we had to move away from Uncle Paul until Laramie pointed out that we could have easily added on in our new custom home because it sat on an acre. But of course, my childhood mind could not even begin to grasp such a thought at the time.

Southern California summers were excruciatingly hot. To fry an egg on the asphalt street was a possibility. But often we would rent a house at the beach for a week or two and enjoy the salty summer swimming in Balboa Bay.

A typical day in hot Whittier was a trip to the Maxime's fabric store.

Julia's Story

Chapter 5
Maxime's Fabrics, Summer 1961

Our mother was not the kind who gave us much advice or even talked to me and my two sisters. She often sat at her place at the round pine dining room table smoking, reading the LA Times or a fiction library book—in silence. Should we come home from school and come up to speak to her about our day we only got a small acknowledgement and a "mmmmmm" murmur from her mouth, as she took a cigarette puff, eyes looking down at the reading material in her hands. She wasn't an easy mother to have, but she was a creative seamstress. It was confusing.

Before school started in the late summer, Mother would take me and my sisters with her on those hot, sweltering Whittier, California afternoons to Maxime's Fabric Store to buy fabric for our school dresses. Way before standard air conditioning, Maxime's was not your prim, organized little fabric store, but, rather, a maze of stacked bolts of factory fabric ends, shoved into piles everywhere on tables, under tables, catastrophically stuffed into the deep narrow storeroom on the main street of Whittier. . . rolls of eyelet, polished cotton, corduroy, seersucker, wool, endless cotton prints. . . .

The air was stagnant, stale and deafening, even though one huge fan worked tirelessly chopping it to no avail. The sun beat from the West through the large plate glass windows only to amplify the dry heat.

This was also way before smoking was taboo, so mother always lit up before she started searching the remnant bolt piles, inhaling the smoke deeply and then releasing it gradually through her nose and mouth. We wandered about for what seemed like hours as mother concentrated trance-like on her purchases. Occasionally she would ask our opinion about a fabric choice, but rarely did we interrupt her, uninvited.

When she was ready, as Maxime began tabbing her out, she'd take one last puff from her current cigarette, drop the cigarette on the floor and step on it just as she was paying the for the sale. We would then haul the huge paper bags of fabrics and notions back to our street-parked heavily chromed 1958 Aqua woody sided Buick Station Wagon, pile into the oven car and head home, hoping the electric windows would open to give us some relief from the heat.

At home, several days later, mother would get to cutting out and sewing together our school dresses from which she often made up her own patterns.

After she cut out and sewed a dress together, she would call, "Julia come put this on so that I can mark the hem!" The dresses were always a perfect fit because she had measured us precisely. Having changed into the new dress, I'd find her settled on the red family room carpet smoking a newly lit cigarette, ashtray nearby, waiting to mark the hem with pins. Each pin mark was perfectly aligned with the floor by a hem-ruler.

"Now turn a little to the left", as she touched me slightly and she pinned the hem mark on the dress.

Over and over, I'd turn slightly as she pinned and over and over she'd touch my legs ever so lightly. Turn pin touch, touch, touch. . .

tickling my mind into a space of timeless bliss.

At one point before she died, when we were alone, I told her about my favorite time with her was when she pinned my new dresses.

One dress, that she designed and created just for me, had a white bibbed apron attached to the dark blue dress. Two white sashes hung to the sides and were to be tied in a bow at my lower back. It was symbolic at the time, but I could not see it until I was much older, and the dress was long gone. I was her helper/servant—the good girl. The other two girls were adrift.

Julia's Story

Chapter 6
My Marriage

When I was still in college, I took a job as a kitchen girl at my parent's favorite dude ranch which was a few miles West of Jackson Hole, Wyoming, under the Tetons. This is where I met my husband-to-be. A tall, charming local boy, worldly of Jackson Hole and that cowboy world. We started dating that summer, then when I returned to college in Oregon, he also returned to Oregon where his family had made a permanent move. They spent winters in Oregon, summers still in Wyoming, so we continued dating and married two years later.

Although our wedding was at my Whittier home, I was determined to settle in Oregon after we married. If I had wanted to move away from my confusing family, I could not explain this even to myself at the time. But today I realized that I wanted to move away from Laramie, in particular. I had no recourse to her unkind words. The day I announced to her that I had a boyfriend, she made fun of his name. At our wedding celebration, she and her husband made it clear that our best man who happened to be a Green Beret was unacceptable to them because they were against the Vietnam war. Me being the good girl wasn't exactly cutting it when Laramie was beyond the pale, always seeking the mean, cutting centerpiece.

Later After I married, to add to the confusion, my retired parents moved three hundred and fifty miles from Whittier to Santa Cruz,

California, in order to live ten miles from Laramie and her husband. All of us were on guard to receive another of her surprise explosive angry outbursts. Why they chose to retire so near Laramie was beyond me. I wanted nothing to do with them all, but of course did not share this. I told them I just wanted to live in Oregon. Uncle Paul

My husband and I had a boy and a girl several years after we married, I taught school most of this time, and he worked on and off as a tradesman. We had our ups and downs. The marriage lasted twenty-three years. After we divorced, I made a solo move to Eugene, Oregon where I live today. Could my propensity to be overhelpful have been a clue to the dissolution of my marriage? Quite possibly.

Chapter 7
Awakening 1986

It was a cold, grey November day in Newport, Oregon 1986. I had just gotten home from teaching first grade. I was exhausted. I was beginning to prepare a fruit salad and hamburgers for our family—my husband, our two children ages 7 and 11 and myself. The nearby hall phone rang. I picked it up. It was my mother calling from Santa Cruz, California where she and my father had moved for retirement.

In an emotionless tone she informed me that "Your father is in the hospital." And went on to add: "Don't come."

It was such a shock I was barely able to speak. I knew he had serious breathing problems after smoking cigarettes most of his life, but I could not imagine why she had told me directly—don't come. No details, no time for questions. The message was that short.

Furthermore, it was not a secret that our mother was not kind to him in his illness. She continued to smoke while he had quit ten years before. It was so uncomfortable to be around them when he needed something and asked "pleeese, will you get me a sandwich" as he sat permanently in his chair at the dining room table, unable to do much for himself, only laboriously breathing. It made no sense—her not wanting me to come down and help, her clear, stoic stay away when I had been the daughter of her three who was usually the most helpful.

Then, after I made a few phone calls out, the first of which was to the nurse in charge of him at the Dominican Hospital in Santa Cruz,

I found that he was probably near his death and that if I wanted to see him, I better come now. I decided to go see him without notifying my mother. He had kindly raised me, loved me, sent me to college and had given me away at my marriage. Our mother was the kingpin, our father was the dutiful husband. He was ever so generous. I owed it to him. I made an airport reservation for the next day out of Portland to San Jose, California. I planned to rent a car, drive to Santa Cruz and then rent a motel room near the hospital. Never mind my mother's request.

The next day at one PM my heart pounded as my plane landed in San Jose, hoping that I had come in time to be there before he died. Arriving at Dominican Hospital, I parked, went in the front doors and I asked the woman at the Hospital desk if my father was still there (alive?).

"Yes, he is here, in room 221".

I took the elevator to the second floor, and I scrambled to find his room, my heart pounded so loud I thought it could be heard, my mouth was dry, and my breath was short with fear.

I found his room and appeared at the door.

"Jew-Ya" my father exclaimed! He was sitting up in his bed in a double room. There was a roommate behind a white curtain breathing on a noisy respirator. We could only hear the heavy breathing machine pumping air in and out from behind the curtain. Dad's eyes were anxious, his breathing hard, laborious, and heavy. His brown eyes were watery and small.

My father was alive, breathing on his own so we could talk.

"Dad, I came to see how you are! Mother told me not to come, so she does not know that I have come," I told him.

We both knew he was dying; his last few years had been laboriously difficult with his inability to breathe. He apologized for his drinking—I forgave him easily. He had always been kind. He asked me a question, "Did I think Uncle Paul, our mother's uncle, did I think that Uncle Paul molested Mother"? It had never occurred to me, but, yes, I told him, because I knew that Uncle Paul molested my little sister Marion. Not giving it much thought, it made sense.

"Yes. I believe that is true, Dad". We shared a good ten minutes when I asked, "Why did mother not want me to come"? –At that moment, Mother walked into his room through the open door, holding his light blue pajamas folded over her left arm.

"Here are the pajamas you asked for. . . ." but when her eyes lit on me, she turned ashen white. Could I not have missed her eyes turning to rage? I had rarely gone intentionally against her word, until this moment.

"Julia!" what are you doing here?" she spewed angrily.

I did not really answer but told her I planned to stay at a motel. In a rush, she quickly put the pajamas down and turned the conversation over to taking me shopping to my favorite bookstore, announcing that I would be staying with her. Nothing about dad. Numb as I was, I followed her out at her request as if in a trance. I thought we might call dad that night.

We did not call dad that night. Nor did anyone call us that night at her house. Neither of my two sisters appeared or called. My parents lived nine miles from Santa Cruz up a winding road into the redwoods. Their white clapboard house overlooked a wandering stream through an old growth patch of redwoods. During dinner in their royal green carpeted living room, overlooking the little stream below the tall old growth redwood trees, even though I felt transfixed by her authority, I wanted to help her. I could not understand why she was acting so irrational around dad's neediest hour. I was familiar with Al-anon. So, thinking that this might help her, I suggested it.

"Mother, Dad is dying, can you not see this? Might you consider Al-anon to help you get through this?"

This was a big mistake. The next morning, after a night of no sleep, I found her sitting at the table, smoking, drinking coffee, and reading the paper. After a few brief words, I suggested Al-Anon again at which time she commanded me:

"How dare you tell me to go to Al-Anon! Leave my house! Leave my house and never come back!"

I had never heard such words from her. Ever. I had finally done something that was truly unforgivable. I had defied her wishes once before, but I never heard her in this tone. Still numb and confused, I gladly threw my things into my suitcase and left in a heartbeat—drove my rental car down the winding road to the hospital, hoping Dad was still alive.

I parked and went directly to his room—only to find it empty. The nurse's station was nearby. I was panicked, but then a nurse redirected me to another private room. He was alone. I refreshed him on the events of that morning. I thanked him for being my father and kissed him. Then, he told me directly, "Go, Julia, go, go!" As if to say get as far away from this family as possible. From this family or. . . . mother. I was not sure.

I begged his nurse at the station to not let him return home, but this was useless. She explained, "Distant family members often try to interfere and had no business doing so."

I had only intentionally defied my mother's wishes once before. It was when I was 23. I came home for my fifth high school class reunion, and she had promised to buy my dress for the occasion. Only when she chose a full-length prairie dress and I chose a more attractive short skirt dress with bodice fitted waist, I decided to buy my own dress. She refused to talk to me the rest of the day, oddly enough. *That* had never happened before.

It would be years before I had a clue to what this was about. Years.

After saying goodbye to my father, I returned to San Jose and got a ticket home to Oregon a day earlier than I had planned. Sitting in a double seat with a woman passenger sitting next to me, we started to talk.

"My father is dying, and my mother just divorced me, sending me away forever". I was numb, in shock. I could not even begin to understand this situation. Luckily, shock was my friend at this time, keeping me contained, though my voice was hollow, my body tranced.

The reason I could not understand this situation is because of her three children, I was the easiest to raise. She wasn't easy to have as a mother, but it was my only recourse to do good in her eyes—to be the good girl who helped her shop for groceries, to always do my homework and get decent grades, to clean up the messy house we lived in. . . . My young family and I even came down the previous summer to help her when she broke her leg, when she had no one but us because Laramie the oldest daughter was estranged. And Marion was traveling in Africa.

The woman sitting next to me hesitated for a moment before she spoke.

"Have you ever heard of narcissism? There is a book called *Trapped in the Mirror: Adult Children of Narcissists in their Struggle for Self* by Elan Glomb PH. D.

I had never heard of the book, nor was I familiar with narcissism, but I was of course curious. When I got back home to Oregon I bought a copy of the book, but this was certainly not a complete answer. It was only a beginning. Narcissism is when a person only thinks of themselves, manipulates others to obey their orders and has little or no empathy.

My father died a few days later at their home, my mother and one sister had gone out shopping and upon return found him no longer alive on the bathroom floor in their house. There was a call to tell me. I was not asked to come nor did I choose to return. It would be years before I could even start to put the puzzle pieces together.

I do remember having sharp abdominal pain in the weeks following. My doctor prescribed valium. It seemed to help momentarily. But the scar of that day was deep and wonting.

There was something amiss for sure. When something in a family doesn't ring, isn't quite right, we start to observe every little nuance, every little dissonance, especially as children we do this. We also look back and start to reevaluate. And often we feel like there is something wrong with us, because the adults in charge give no mention to the quirky incident that slid out of the cracks. But I was not going to forget this.

At a much later date Laramie told me that she went to see our dad the day after I returned home. He told her to "GET OUT!".

Chapter 8
Mother's Goodness

I was utterly confused because my mother had been the most interesting mother of all the mothers I knew. Mother was a natural artist, she had decorated our home to be magazine ready with a colorful red-themed wall papered front family room. She also decorated the adjacent living room with varying shades of blue, centered with a light pink couch. She encouraged us to do our own arts and crafts projects, giving us Indian bead sets, paints, clay, yarn, and craft books. Plus, she never really complained about our after-craft messes. Her kitchen was always open for us to experiment making cookies or cake.

She provided board games—Monopoly, Clue Parcheesi, and Chutes and Ladders. She willingly shared her sewing room and sewing machine with us—as well as all her abundant fabric stock. Periodicals such as *Time Magazine, Life, Saturday Evening Post, Sunset and Vogue* streamed through our Whittier house endlessly. The bookshelves burgeoned with books. Regular library trips brought more books home. She read many books to us—like *Mary Poppins, Charlotte's Web,* and *Stewart Little.*

She and dad took us to dude ranches in Colorado and California. She drove us to horseback riding, swimming, and girl scout events. And she took us camping to many major Western United States Campgrounds, as well as to downtown LA film openings like *Oklahoma, South Pacific, The King and I,* and *Sound of Music.*

However, with all these incredible offers, there was one problem that we did not really acknowledge until much later. Mother couldn't manage Laramie's unreasonably defiant behavior.

I first noticed when Laramie had problems in school. She could not read at the pace the teacher and mother expected her to read in first grade. Mother had taught herself to read when she was three or four, she told us. I watched mother trying to teach Laramie to read on the daybed in the dining room when we lived in the apartment above the family business. Tears streamed down Laramie's face under this duress.

Then, when we moved to Whittier, I remember seeing Laramie regularly crying before school started at her classroom door, mother standing by her, her not wanting to go into her 5th grade classroom. School phobia was mentioned as a possible reason, but then other troubles came into the picture as she aged. Freshman year of high school she flunked out, so to speak, or did not attend to her assignments, so in order to remedy the situation, Mother sent her to a coed boarding school, from which she was eventually asked to leave as well because of her unruly behavior.

I thought I noticed her ignoring me when we were in grade school together—when I waved to get her attention on the playground she would not respond. I wasn't sure.

Laramie was unknowingly affecting me indirectly because in fifth grade I became obsessed with thinking that I was a bad girl when being a bad girl was the farthest from the truth. I was too good, trying to balance out the negative energy Laramie was creating in our family. At one point, I imagined that I had cancer and that no one was telling me. They were keeping a secret from me. Mother had to come to school to take me home early because I couldn't stop crying, thinking this thought. When I told her what I was worried about, she took me to the doctor and he said, "There is nothing wrong with her". Secrets seep, but at that time in my life, I hadn't a clue what was happening with me. Insanity might have been a possibility.

Laramie failed her first year of high school and Mother sent her to a co-ed boarding school in the Mountains, but she failed there as well. Her behavior was unruly and bizarre. She snuck into the boys dormitory one night and drew lipstick on their faces.

When she returned home to my high school, I wasn't sure, I noticed her intentional effort to ignore me as we passed in the halls. She wouldn't respond to my "Hi Laramie" greeting, then she would walk quickly past me with a witch-like walk, marching her feet and flailing her arms.

 We had little to do with each other at home as well. We never shared friends. I learned only recently that because Laramie was eight years older than Marion, she taught Marion to hate both me and our mother. So, Marion was equally unavailable to me. I had not a clue why she tried to ignore me as well.

Laramie became more vocal, hating me and our mother for no apparent reason. She was the elephant in the room, so to speak, so I did my best to be helpful to balance out this odd energy that we were all trying to ignore. My efforts were lifelong until I left the house and married.

Eventually after I had visited our dad in the hospital, Laramie and I spoke on the phone. I shared what Dad had mentioned about mother being molested. In this conversation, Laramie explained to me that we must have had to move away from Great Uncle Paul because we could have added onto the house we already built to make more room for new born baby Marion. "You mean that Uncle Paul is Marion's father?". This reality could only come slowly to me. She further added that Great Uncle Luther was her father. I never knew Luther because he died soon after I was born. His name was mentioned in family conversation on occasion.

My two sisters biologically related to our grandmother's brother-in-law and her brother. It would be a while before I could ingest this possibility. Laramie further went on to suggest my biological mother was our Great Aunt Ruth who was sixty years old when I was born. It was all too much for me, but I remembered moving away from Great Uncle Paul and had remembered Marion telling me much later that he fondled her sexually when she was very small. I couldn't be sure about any of it.

When I was about to be married, Laramie came to my wedding celebration and immediately spoke out against our best man. She wanted it known that she was against the Vietnam war, he was a Green Beret in uniform, so she was against him—she announced in her rude awakening way. It was like she could always throw a grenade into any family gathering in order to throw attention her way—even on my wedding day. This was her continued lifelong practice—to create an uproar.

Mother did her best to deal with Laramie's continued outbursts, starting when Laramie turned thirteen, to no avail. Much later in 2003 when we heard that mother had only a few weeks to live, Laramie came to "help out" only to spend time confiscating Mother's prescribed marijuana and pain medication.

Mother always provided for us even though Laramie was beyond the pale. Mother could only teach us to learn to ignore and accept Laramie—without reason.

McKinney Homestead

Chapter 9
Laura Julia Baskett and Charlie Columbus

I tried to stop my detective work investigation, to no avail. Could my father's comment about my mother being molested, have to do with my two sisters having different fathers? Was it something about our maternal family? I wasn't sure, so I continued this insidious search.

Great-grandmother Laura Julia was born in 1868 in McKinney, Texas. Her father was a settler from England, and granted 640 acres to develop and settle, soon after the Apache Indians had finished terrorizing the white settlers who were invading their land. She was born just after the United States Civil war ended. Her father had built a long ranch house with a covered porch.

Laura Julia married Charlie Columbus Basket, a neighbor farm boy, when she was 16, and the two of them tried to make a living on the 40 acres her father bequeathed to her.

She spoke of living on poke greens for two years and having to pick cotton with the Blacks, one baby on her back the other in her body to make ends meet. Charlie Columbus was no farmer and he eventually got a job on the Southern Pacific Railroad which was just coming to their town. He was a brakeman from that day until he retired.

The railroad gave his growing family free train rides. Their first train-ride was a move to Fresno, California where the railroad put them in company housing. Charlie was rarely at home. My grandmother remembers hobos marking their house as one that gave food to starving travelers. There were signs that previous hobos scratched in dirt to notify other hobos of possible offerings. Although they had little to offer, they always gave something to a begging stranger. A fish drawn in the dirt indicated: food here. A circle drawn in the dirt: good place. A cross drawn in the dirt: religious talk, free meal.

While Great-grandmother had only an 8th grade education, she managed to feed and clothes her growing family of five children by sewing their clothes, gardening, keeping chickens and always cooking from scratch. Charlie Columbus was rarely home. Because Grandmother Chapman was the most responsible/reliable child, of the five, she was responsible for "the brood" while her mother was tending to house work for everyone.

Once, when I discovered alcoholism in my own marriage, I asked my grandmother, "Did your father drink?"

"No, he was a tea-totaler", she told me. However, I didn't quite believe her because my mother had told me he never graduated past railroad brakeman his whole life. It was the lowest railroad job. He was also known to fall asleep on the job. Charlie Columbus didn't have much interaction with his family either. Although, he did play the mandolute and was often sent off to play checkers with the grandchildren while the adult family members visited in the parlor.

Always renting, with not much furniture to fill the houses great-grandmother Laura Julia ended up renting a little bungalow on Bernardo Street near Chinatown in Los Angeles. The street still exists today, huddled up against the Los Angeles Angels Stadium. No furniture in the front room at the time my Grandmother Chapman was in high school she told me.

Here are the things I knew of great-grandmother when I was very small. . . . . she made cheap treats of cupcakes topped with white frosting sprinkled with crushed Christmas candy. She once put my hair up in "rags" to curl it when I was four years old. She always had a cardboard box of candy bars high on the top shelf of her closet kitchen pantry to share when we went to visit her in her and Auntie Ruth's home. Butterfinger was my favorite.

On Easter when the family came to our Whittier house for Easter breakfast of eggs goldenrod (hardboiled egg whites in white sauce on buttered toast sprinkled with hardboiled, sieved egg yokes) she brought elaborate Easter baskets for me and my sisters. She bought "five and dime" jellybeans and chocolate bunnies and wrapped the baskets in pink cellophane tied together with thick blue ribbons.

She and Auntie Ruth had no car nor television. Uncle Paul was their shopping driver-man and garden lawn mower. Christian Science literature eventually turned into phonograph records as Laura Julia became blind—all laid out on their dining room mahogany table. Even though they lived on an urban street in the city of Whittier she and Great Aunt Ruth kept un-cooped banty hens wandering their back yard.

She had a round belly as if she were pregnant at age 90. Mother thought it must have been a neglected benign tumor. My great-grandmother Laura Julia always wore a red sweater with pockets—a flowered hankie in the right pocket. Was that the scent of roses I smelled as she dabbled her nose? She wore a red sweater over her dress and wore thick stockings and old lady lace-up shoes. She did not go to doctors that I know of, but probably only called Christian Science Practitioners.

The exception to this is, I believe, they took her to the hospital when she broke her hip when she was nearly one hundred years old, but only after she clung to the side of her bed for several days probably having Christian Science literature read to her by a practitioner. She was in the hospital shortly before she died, just before her hundredth birthday 1967.

After her death, they found $17,000 hidden in her room under her mattress. At holiday gatherings, I watched her give mother a hundred dollar bill to pay for the turkey or whatever. I wondered later if she took the bill from her bedroom stash.

Also, as she became blind, she used to enjoy feeling the fabric of our dresses. I wanted her to learn braille, but Grandmother Chapman told me she was too old for that.

One cousin of my mother's generation told me that Charlie Columbus was almost a non-member of the household. "Go take the children off to play checkers" (so that the adults can talk family business). Charlie Columbus was mostly not home to raise the five children. His last name was Baskett because as a baby, he was found left in a basket at someone's door. Someone took him in. I never met him but got the impression that he was disregarded by family similarly to Grandfather Chapman. Whenever his name was mentioned at family gatherings, it was in a zestful sing-song tone. Of course, if this was true it was never mentioned to me by my Grandmother Chapman.

Chapter 10
Christian Science

"There is nothing either good or bad but thinking makes it so." — Shakespeare

Mary Baker Eddy's picture hung framed in Laura Julia Baskett's bedroom. The above quote is on the first page of Mary Baker Eddy's book *Science and Health with key to the Scriptures* by Mary Baker. I don't know why Great-grandmother Laura Julia became a member of this church, except that I did hear that she suffered health problems while raising her five children and gave the responsibility of taking care of her children to my grandmother, who was the most reliable one of the five.

Each of her five children followed her lead in reading the assigned daily lessons Mrs. Eddy created. The Bible and Mrs. Eddy's book *Science and Health* were on the table in their parlors laid out to be read each day. Thus, no doctors for any of them. You were *to work it out with science* or call a Christian Science practitioner to help you work it out, should you deem yourself "sick". We were told that sickness was just in your imagination as you were actually a perfect creation of God. Going to the doctor meant that you did not believe "good-enough" that you were perfectly well. If you thought you were sick, it was a problem with your thinking.

Julia's Story

So be it. Grandmother Chapman gave each of my sisters and I color-coded Christian Science book sets. Mine were green. I was the only grandchild who used these books. At high school age, I had a Christian Science teacher at the local Christian Science Church where I went alone to Sunday School. My teacher claimed to have healed from cancer.

I was also a counselor at a Christian Science camp in the San Jacinto Mountains above Palm Springs for five full summers. The camp leaders were not purists, because some of the campers were not of this religion, but we got short Christian Science lectures on occasional Sundays.

Christian Science Journal Magazine lists endless healings through "Science". So, before the advent of pollution and high stress, this was the elder family mantra. Except, when it did not work as in when Luther had an appendicitis attack and went to the family mountain cabin to "work it out with Science" and never came back. His brother, Herschel, had a heart condition that took his life. Then their father Charlie Columbus Baskett died as well within the same few years before 1950. The Baskett women, namely Laura Julia Basket, Grandmother Chapman and Auntie Fredda and Auntie Ruth outlasted all the men—living into their 90's if not 100 years old—without doctors.

This all left an impression on me. The possibility that there was something about our thinking that created our life experience. However, in my mother's home, we always went to the family doctor, got immunization shots, and when my mother had cancer during her pregnancy with Marion she had an operation to have her cancerous rib bone removed. We didn't play around with our health. But we also didn't have such over-the-counter remedies as aspirin in our home. The neighbor girl whose father was a doctor had to go home from playing one day, because she had a headache and needed an aspirin.

"You have a what? And you need a what?" I had no idea what she was talking about because we didn't have that language at home. A small blessing.

But it was interesting that this pious family, all members born before the turn of the century, made it clear that one's thinking affected one's life. *THIS* was certainly something to hold on to, in my opinion. And this formula of thinking was a beginning for me when I started obsessing about something after I was divorced, like my new boyfriend who was married.

So, with Christian Science in mind, I made little affirmation cards to remind me of and help me know better realities. If repeated lessons from Mary Baker Eddy worked, why would my own reality cards not work? These affirmations were not from *Science and Health* by Mary Baker Eddy but from popular new age authors like Deepak Chopra. Examples were, *"Be who you are"*, ... I kept this little 3 by 4 inch packet of hand written cards with me at all times and pulled them out while waiting in a long line or sitting in an office for an appointment.

I had taught public elementary school for 17 years before my divorce, so I decided to quit teaching for good (which never happened until I retired in 2003) and take some time to open a metaphysical bookstore in the small Oregon coast town where I lived. I had a partner for a while and we named the store Warm Regards. It is where I began to acknowledge and hone my intuition skills and where I learned to give tarot readings—which led to authentic psychic readings (I have to say here not all psychic readings are authentic, there are plenty of scammers, just like in any profession.)The bookstore lasted two years, I closed the store, sold the building, and moved to another town away from my former life.

Julia's Story

Chapter 11
New Life New Awareness

I moved to Eugene, Oregon alone, to go back to college and had to drop out the first term. At age 50, I was not a fit in the MBA program at University of Oregon. I had to go back to teaching because it was my only means of cash flow. I still had the obsessive thinking problem of being in love with an unavailable man, so, I also began seeing a Jungian Psychotherapist—Dr. Sylvia Weishaupt. I thought I could use her services for a year, which turned into thirteen years.

I had already worked to change my thinking by reading new age books and by creating affirmation cards but Sylvia offered a different and far more intriguing bent: Jungian Psychotherapy where we began to examine my dreams and the unconscious aspect of myself. It was through this therapy that my unconscious began to become known to me. Gradually, my dreams enhanced my original search of why my mother had disowned me as my father lay dying. Today, I have over 40 filled dream journals and still write my dreams routinely. She also helped me see the *good girl complex* that I fell into to survive my childhood. Complexes such as this one never disappear, she told me, but it helps to become aware of my tendency to try to please.

Thus, in this memoir, you will notice I use natural curiosity, dreams and some psychic information to tell parts of my story.

I started noticing my dreams. Many dreams stood out, but one dream began helping me understand my family situation:

I am standing at the driveway entrance to my childhood home in Whittier, I notice that there is another group of people living in the same house, only they are living one floor below us. I had never noticed this before, but I see that there are lights on and the area is being lived in.

Was this the other family story that I had not known all the while when I was growing up in that house? Was it the invisible second story?
There was another dream.

I am at my Great-grandmother Laura Julia Baskett's gingerbread-like painted house with dark brown shutters. My father and I are outside speaking to her on the front walk. There is a key on the walk.

My father never visited her house in my memory. This dream had to do with a key connection between my father and Great-grandmother Laura Julia Baskett, which comes up later in this story.
I became involved in the Eugene Jung group in town that brought lectures to our city by Jungian speakers. I also visited Switzerland and spent two weeks there one hot summer taking classes on Jungian Psychotherapy in 2001 in Zurich.
Without any intention on my part, my Jungian Psychotherapy began to slide into helping me solve my family mystery as my love problem with the unavailable man began to diminish.

Chapter 12
Mother's Passing

Our mother died November 11, 2003, at 84 years old. I am the middle of her three daughters. By this time, her youngest daughter Marion lived almost next door to her on a street in Santa Cruz, California. Upon notification of mother's illness, I flew from Eugene, Oregon to help Marion with the doctors' appointments and hospital details. Our older sister Laramie came to apparently help but spent much of her visit locating mother's medical marijuana prescription for herself. She had been somewhat estranged from the family, although she also lived in California, but in nearby Arroyo Grande.

Nonetheless, the three of us were the recipients of an extraordinary childhood in that we each had our own room in a beautiful house in Southern California. Our mother and Grandmother Chapman treated us to the best clothes, our parents gave us fabulous Christmases, we rode horses, went swimming, were taken on vacations to the beach, to Western Dude Ranches, and were taken to all the National Parks to camp. We went to white-only schools. We were even each given a brand-new car by Grandmother Chapman after high school. Our college was fully paid for. We apparently had it all. And I must say that we were less than appreciative as rich kids sometimes are. In my defense, it is all we knew.

So, upon arrival to mother's hospital room in Santa Cruz, we still did not know her diagnosis. We just knew that she couldn't swallow very well and had terrible stomach pain. We asked the hospital nurse when we could speak to the doctor.

She told us, "The doctor comes early in the morning, so better be in her room by 5:30 AM or you might miss him."

The next morning we did just that.

The doctor's diagnosis was short and pat: Metastasized lung cancer that had already traveled to her liver. She was a lifelong smoker, so this was no surprise. He gave her six months to live with treatment, and less time without. She chose no treatment.

Upon hearing this news, Marion and mother cried silently. I don't know if Laramie cried. By that time, mother and I had lost our connection. I had been her only child-helper in our growing-up years. Her other two daughters were more difficult to raise. Laramie was a hateful bully and Marion refused to talk to mother by Laramie's command for two years when Laramie and I were out of the house going to college. But at this time, Marion had become estranged from Laramie and had become mother's side-kick helper.

After our father died in 1986, when I attempted to reconnect with mother on many occasions, I was often recoiled without rational cause. She never explained her behavior around dad's death, and I never asked her to explain it. I carried the sharp abdominal pain of this disconnection as if a knife had been sharply stabbed into my gut, then twisted, but it had been fifteen years since this event of my father's death and the pain had tamped down, knowing I might never know why she had told me to leave and never return. My sisters were mum.

We ordered a hospital bed to be put in the living area of her house, and once we all settled back into her home, I decided to spend my time sewing together a Wool Swiss-style jacket. I bought some thick ivory wool fabric, a jacket pattern, and 8 silver antique buttons. I sat on the floor next to mother's hospital bed cutting and sewing my jacket for the duration of my week stay. She had little to say. I dared not ask her anything at this point. But I told her, "My favorite time with you was when you hemmed my dresses. I loved the tickling of the skirt as I turned and you pinned it." My last words to her as I left after a week, were "You are going to be ok. You will just be fine. Do not worry about it", I told her. I had no tears as I walked away.

"OK if you say so, " she responded.

She passed a few days later.

Julia's Story

Chapter 13
The Journal And Photo Discovery

In 2015, twelve years after mother's passing, Marion invited me to come see how she had moved into mother's house. As I walked through the front hall and into the living area, I noticed a stack of photos and memorabilia about 10 inches high on mother's round, worn pine dining room table.

"What's this", I asked?

Marion responded, "Oh just a bunch of old family stuff that I am going to throw away. You can go through it and take what you want before I toss it all out."

There were several old photos of mother's family members, as well as the photo of a large upscale two-story house I had never seen, with a lovely, maintained rolling front lawn. There was also a scripted insignia written in pencil on the back: Laura Baskett's Rampart House!

And there was also a small 4" by 7" black leather-bound booklet sewn roughly with black sewing machine stitches. I opened it to discover some yellowed lined paper that had been hand sewn onto the leather booklet cover. The word "TRUST" is barely scratched on the middle front cover. Inside, in red pencil, the hand-written words "a will" is written. And the earliest date written is put on the first page: 23rd of Feb 1916. It was in my great-grandmother's beautiful, scripted writing. 95% of it correct spelling (the teacher in me noticed).

I didn't stop to read much more at the time because I didn't want to seem too curious. Marion was clearly not interested in our past.

Julia's Story

But I took it home to Oregon after my sister-visit, along with the photo of the big house. At home in Oregon, I began paging through this homemade booklet, reading each page carefully to find a treasure of information I could hardly believe.

I will spare you the entire hand-written journal. In summary, it was written in script by Great-grandmother Laura Julia Baskett when she was 48 years old in contemplation of her maiden daughter Ruth's need for money after Laura Julia and Charlie Columbus died. Life expectation at the time of 1916 had been 40 or 50 years.

At first Laura Julia puts in $1522.21 explaining that is all she has to put into Ruth's Trust. February 1916. She starts listing the 6% semi-annual interest she receives from the Trust Investor, Mr. Griffith in these amounts: $47.31, $46.24, $46.27, ... until December 1918.

Then in December 1919 she gives the investor $2,500 more. A month later she puts in $10,000 more. In 1920 a small house costs $800. A loaf of bread costs 10 cents. Eventually, she increases this amount eight different times and her total on April 13, 1931 is $21,000.

I looked up the address of the Rampart house in the photo and found the house to still be standing in a part of Los Angeles. It is the same house as in the photo, only it has been converted into a duplex today. It appears to originally have 5 or more bedrooms.

This was a discovery to behold.

A few years before this discovery I had spoken to a local psychic about there possibly being prostitution in my Grandmother Chapman's early life. Laramie had suggested this to me ten or more years previous. I pictured my Great-grandmother offering herself for money in her modest rental in order to feed her five children.

"No. It is quite a large brothel with many bedrooms and the girls inside, are they Chinese?," she asked me?

"And were there drugs?" I asked.

"Yes", she answered.

I filed this information away as unbelievable, just as I had at first heard Laramie tell me about the two Great Uncles. Grandmother Chapman's family members were pius Christian Scientists. None of the women were overly made up. It was unfathomable to me.

Rampart House
1916

Julia's Story

Chapter 14
Putting The Pieces Together

Grandmother Chapman's brother Herschel Baskett became the foreign traveling salesman for Burroughs Adding Machines in the first three decades of the twentieth century. He traveled by ship across oceans to Asian countries like China, India, and the Philippines. I imagine that he was able to sell the mechanical adding machines to former abacus users, but that is just my guess. Herschel was also known to send home large carved wooden trunks full of souvenirs from his travels. My grandmother Chapman's home displayed so many of these souvenirs—small carved statues of rose quartz and ivory, hand-sewn wall-size Chinese tapestries that hung on Grandmother's hall walls as well as Chinese Ming vases on her display shelves.

Could Grandmother Chapman have married Burk, her deaf husband, to access his import business? Could Herschel possibly have sent home opium in the trunks along with souvenirs? There were surly opium dens in Chinatown Los Angeles in these decades. Did he send other imported drugs? Could the photo of this large Rampart Street home be the brothel that a local psychic informed me even before I happened on the photo? How did my great-grandmother become so wealthy? How did my grandmother acquire so many properties?

Something else, many years before I had my own children, in my early marriage, during a visit to Grandmother Chapman's home, Grandmother handed me a wood-burned box with some images she explained that she and her sisters wood-burned onto the top and sides when they were teenagers. I took it home and put it away. I had never noticed the images on this box before, but now I noticed the burned woman image on the top of the box seemed to be happily enjoying herself, while poppy flower images surrounded her. Might these poppies have been opium poppies? The opium box image is on the cover of this book.

And why would my beautiful, intellectual, educated Grandmother Chapman marry a deaf, uneducated boy-man eight years her senior? Could it have been the convenience of his chinaware import business at a time when Los Angeles ports were just beginning to make laws about illegal drug trafficking—while Herschel was traveling the world? Might my Great-grandmother Laura Julia's tight knit family have been similarly likened to a Mafia family, except for their Christian Science devotion? And what about all those Los Angeles properties Grandmother Chapman owned?

And what about our familiarity with Chinatown dinners? Could my great-grandmother Laura Julia Baskett have been an honorary madame sitting at the restaurant table head? And how could her family of five children so poor that there was no furniture in the living room when my grandmother Chapman was a teenager (1905 she was 16)—how could this family, living on a railroad brakeman salary be so suddenly rich?

As I was gathering this information, I had remembered the dream of my father and Great-grandmother Laura Julia meeting outside her house. There was a key on the sidewalk between them—did my father continue to import drugs in the family business while my sisters and I were still growing up? Again this was unfathomable to me. However, our parents' retirement years were filled with exotic travels to Japan, the South Seas, and Africa. Mother also had an acquaintance who created expensive, exorbitant jewelry in these years. They were also very chummy with their Japanese agents who imported their chinaware. My parents made many trips to Japan as well as invited their Japanese agents to come stay with them in their home in the Redwoods, always exchanging gifts and kindnesses with these kind men.

I might assume that our family money came from three places: the import chinaware business, the sale of drugs, and the sale of drug-laundered LA properties my Grandmother Chapman gradually sold off.

The many properties that my grandmother's family owned starting in the 1920's, were certainly more than most people owned at this time in US History: a mountain Cabin on Mount Baldy, a beach home on Balboa Island, the Victorian house/turned business-apartment, the houses in this neighborhood where Grandpa collected rents, and the lovely downtown Los Angeles home where mother lived as a child and teenager. There was also the large, many bedroomed two story home in the photograph I took from Marion's stack of throw-away mementos.

Most interestingly, all members of this tight-knit family were sober, non-smoking Christian Scientists, except my parents and our Great Uncle Paul who was never considered a member of "the family". Might my Grandmother Chapman have been the family fiduciary? She would have had to have known about laundering illegal money through the purchase of property—way before Donald Trump came around. When I finally disobeyed my mother when she told me to not come to see my father—might my mother have been afraid that my father would tell me ***this*** family secret?

Might Great-grandmother Laura Julia and Grandmother Chapman have done this at a time when women and children had little priority? Women were first allowed to vote in the year 1919 (the African Americans weren't allowed until 1957)? Property ownership by women was also a problem. Grandmother might had gotten her deaf husband to sign on to new property without much fuss. He did whatever she asked.

I inherited six, fourteen-caret gold scrimshaw (design etched) bracelets from Grandmother Chapman's trove. Somehow these bracelets all ended up with me. I have no memory of why they all came to me, but I am sure such expensive jewelry was not common in brakeman salaried homes.

However, can I not see how their early twentieth century living on the edge, first having to pick cotton and eat poke greens on the high Texas prairie, then living in low- income three-room bungalows in Chinatown, might have sharpened their thirst for wealth. Once the money began to flow, they all apparently owned gold scrimshaw bracelets because this batch came to me when I was beyond innocent of where such jewelry might occur. And, apparently they soon learned to shop at the best department stores in downtown Los Angeles. My sisters and I were the lucky recipients of their need to buy the best school clothing for us.

Eventually, everyone in this family acquired above average custom-built houses or better. Great Uncle Paul and Grandmother Chapman and my father always drove new cars and owned large properties of gardens and orchards.

As a child, we did not learn to question or debate with the adults. We were just told what was to be. Once when I was about six years old, I asked my grandmother a question: "Why do your two daughters (my mother being one of them) not visit or even like each other?"

She told me, "Never ask this question again!"

It was the same at my home, don't ask any questions, just do what you are told to do. So, it never dawned on me to question any of this until I went against my mother's word at age forty and took a jet down to see my father before he died—when he suggested Uncle Paul might have something to do with molestation of mother, reminding me I already had heard something of this earlier, and that I already knew Paul had molested Marion when she was two or three. It took a while, but I began to see that Uncle Paul might be Marion's biological father. When DNA came to the fore, we never did a DNA test. Marion did not want to this.

Much later, like in the last few years, Laramie again came up with the possibility, that *Great Uncle Luther* was her father because she finally admitted that she had memories of being left with him and of him letting her wear his Schreiner's hat with the bobbing front tassel. *She had memories of him molesting her as well,* before I was born, so she now reported. I doubted her.

I did finally ask our mother if this was true about Marion and Laramie in 1994 and she denied it, but two years later, she sent Laramie a hand typed letter telling her about Luther in a long paragraph. Not admitting his fidelity but giving her this information about her possible biological father who died two years after she was born. Might Great Uncle Paul and Great Uncle Luther have fathered my sisters? I'll never know for sure, but my father hinting this about Great Uncle Paul on his death bed stays with me.

I have no true knowledge of why Laramie was so difficult to live with for my 18 years as her younger sister or why she never really seemed to fit into the general world without making a ruckus about something that offended her or about something more she needed that she wasn't getting. Might a family prostitution business have influenced the young family males to abuse the children of the family? Were the pioneer settler children preyed on by their fathers?

I have had some direct phone and text contact with Laramie this past year and have decided to not engage with her anymore. At seventy-eight she is managing her life in her home in California. She has yet to quiet the fires of her hating our mother and me, of her blaming anyone but herself for her problems. My thirteen years of psychotherapy with Sylvia certainly enhanced my self-confidence. It was difficult being Laramie's sister, but I have overcome the need to nurture her happiness.

A number of reasons could explain mother's need to disown me on that terrible day. The family roots in drug importation could explain her fear of my father telling me about the actual source of our wealth, family prostitution, and my two half sisters.

Secrets are never secret. They seep. Whether I was a fifth grader or a 40-year-old, I noticed something awry. Sealed lips were common. We did not learn to argue because it was silently forbidden. My mother and Grandmother Chapman's lips were sealed, to thir graves, but they also did their best to provide for me and my sisters a most interesting childhood. For whatever reason my Grandmother Chapman and Mother were put into these situations, it appears they had no choice at times when women had so little choice, compared to one hundred years later—today

This was my journey. My good-girl complex served me as a child in this confusing household until I married and had to rethink how this behavior did not serve me anymore. I have since learned to defend my needs. My thirteen-year Jungian Therapy with Dr. Sylvia Weisshaupt helped me understand where I came from and who I am today. It opened a whole new understanding of my family's antics and what affected me in my formative years. It also opened up the world of dreams which I still often record to see what they might tell me. I have also developed an intuition that I never even knew existed. I trust it now.

I also finally had an inkling of why my mother told me to leave and never return. And I now do not have to repeat the past with my own two adult children. For that I am thankful.

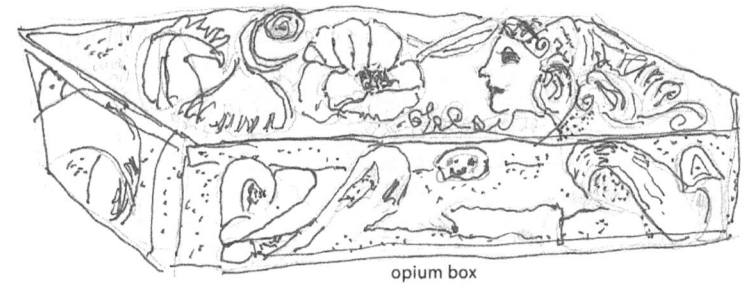
opium box

Chapter 15
Secrets Seep

Secrets that live in family homes seep unknowingly into intuitive children like me. One memorable disturbance was my obsessing over being a bad girl when I was anything but a bad girl. I learned through therapy much later in life that I had the good-girl complex in a home where there were disturbing behaviors by at least another child, my older sister Laramie, who was rarely brought to count. I commiserated silently over being mentally ill with these obsessive thoughts. I find out several decades later that Laramie and Marion had a secret pact to hate me and our mother. They were eight years apart and Laramie had intentionally become Marion's second mother.

Secrets also seep through dreams. I have a dream much later in life that there is another family living underneath our living room/kitchen/dining room. There are lights on through these basement windows and other people are living there at the time we are inhabiting the home. I never noticed this when I lived there. Now I see the elder family story was ingrained in our own family story.

I had a puzzle dream while at Marion/Mother's house after being physically sick the night before. I thought I had been sick by just being in mother's house again after her death. The dream was something about a mixed up pile of puzzle pieces on the floor of the living room, and something about tools rolling around in a box inside a nearby-cabinet.

After this dream, I awoke early at 5:00 AM and got out of bed and began searching the rooms that were in this dream. I opened the cabinet in the front hall to find a box of 360 letters someone has saved 1944 through 1947. They are war letters written by my mother and my father and a few letters written from our grandmothers. Reading them, I find another story of their lives that had been hidden. Tools. My father had saved the letters.

Secrets seep in another way. I was the lone detective in this search for meaning. It was useless to get anyone to help me. I wonder now that I might have foreshadowed my future mystery search when I was twelve years old by reading so many Nancy Drew Mysteries. Nancy Drew detects a mystery and finds the answers within the covers of each book. However, when I had a clue like the wood burned box my Grandmother Chapman gave me in my twenties, I could not or did not see the meaning of the images burned on the top of the box until I connected opium with the flowers. I was never a drug user, so opium flowers were not meaningful to me. Even though I find a clue, it sometimes takes me a while to converge with the meaning. This realization took decades.

So, secrets seep, and are there for you to unveil them, but it takes considerable effort to persevere. Truthfully, I stopped seeking answers many times when I was discouraged by a family member—but, always picking it up again.

End

www.ingramcontent.com/pod-product-compliance
Lightning Source LLC
Chambersburg PA
CBHW041132110526
44592CB00020B/2778